Crochet

Learn to crochet
six great projects

Anne Akers Johnson

KLUTZ®

creates activity books and other great stuff for kids ages 3 to 103. We began our corporate life in 1977 in a garage we shared with a Chevrolet Impala. Although we've outgrown that first office, Klutz galactic headquarters remains in Palo Alto, California, and we're still staffed entirely by real human beings. For those of you who collect mission statements, here's ours:

Create wonderful things • *Be good* • *Have fun*

WRITE US

We would love to hear your comments regarding this
or any of our books. We have many!

KLUTZ®

450 Lambert Avenue
Palo Alto, CA 94306

Book printed in China. All materials manufactured in China.

Distributed in the UK by Scholastic UK Ltd
Westfield Road, Southam, Warwickshire, England CV47 0RA

Distributed in Australia by
Scholastic Australia Customer Service
PO Box 579, Gosford, NSW Australia 2250

ISBN-10: 1-57054-870-6
ISBN-13: 978-1-57054-870-3

4 1 5 8 5 7 0 8 8

VISIT OUR WEBSITE

You can check out all the stuff we make, find a nearby retailer, request a catalog, sign up for a newsletter, e-mail us or just goof off!
www.klutz.com

Basics

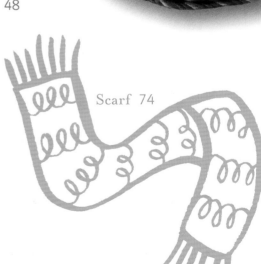

Projects

Basics

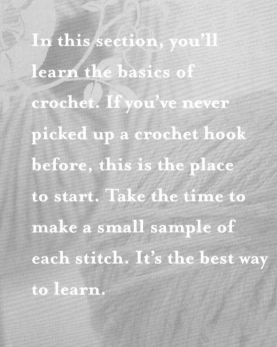

In this section, you'll learn the basics of crochet. If you've never picked up a crochet hook before, this is the place to start. Take the time to make a small sample of each stitch. It's the best way to learn.

What comes with this book

This book comes with everything you need to start crocheting right away.

DK weight yarn

The teal yarn that comes with this book is DK (double knit) weight. There's enough to make most of the small projects, but the scarf will use up all of the yarn. Because the smaller projects are easier, you'll do best if you start with them and shop for new yarn when you're ready to make the scarf.

Button

You'll need this to finish the envelope purse.

Lightweight yarn

The periwinkle yarn is a little thinner than the DK. Use it to make the soap bag. You'll have enough left over to make a flower or two as well.

Ruler

There's a ruler printed on the inside back cover of this book.

4.0 mm crochet hook

This hook will work with both of the yarns that come with this book. When you're buying hooks, always look for the correct size in millimeters.

Stitch markers

Use these when you want to mark the position of a particular stitch. You'll need them to make the hat.

Yarn needle

Use this special needle to sew your projects together.

You'll also need:

Scissors (small ones are fine)
An ordinary needle and thread to sew the button onto the envelope purse

Caring for your yarn

Both of these yarns are 100% viscose. If you want to clean a finished project, simply wash it by hand in cool water then lay it flat to dry. Don't put it in the dryer and never iron it.

Winding yarn

The yarn that comes with this book is wrapped into skeins. When your yarn comes this way (which it often does) you'll need to wrap it into a ball before you use it. If you try to crochet without doing this, you'll end up with a big, tangled mess.

A skein of yarn looks like this:

Carefully pull the skein apart. You'll see that it's a big circle of yarn tied together at some point. Untie or cut the yarn that holds the skein together...

...then carefully drape the skein over the back of a chair as shown in the picture. This will keep it from tangling as you wind.

Hold the end of the yarn with your thumb, then wrap the yarn around two fingers about 10 times.

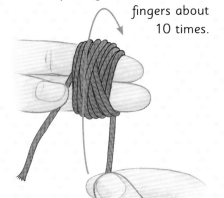

Take the yarn off your fingers, turn it and wrap in a different direction as shown in the picture.

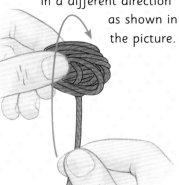

Wind the yarn like this maybe 6 or 7 times...

...then turn the ball of yarn again and make a few more wraps in a different direction. Continue to wrap the yarn every which way to make a nice round ball.

Most yarn stores will wind your yarn free of charge. Be sure to ask.

How to hold your hands

Right-handed crocheters

Yarn hand

about 6 inches long

1 Hold the yarn in your **right** hand, about 6 inches (15 cm) from the end. Wrap the yarn over and around your **left** pinkie...

...up over your two middle fingers...

2 ...and behind your first finger, like so:

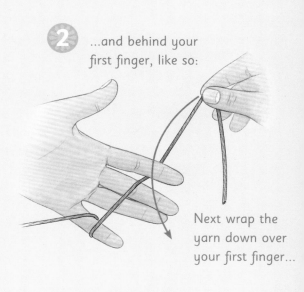

Next wrap the yarn down over your first finger...

Left-handed crocheters

Yarn hand

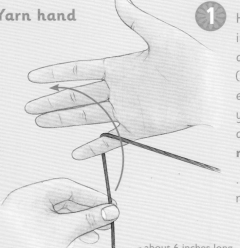

about 6 inches long

1 Hold the yarn in your **left** hand, about 6 inches (15 cm) from the end. Wrap the yarn over and around your **right** pinkie...

...up over your two middle fingers...

2 ...and behind your first finger, like so:

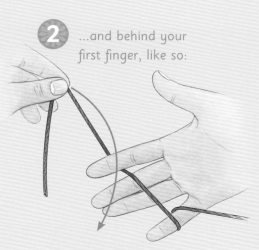

Next wrap the yarn down over your first finger...

...and pinch it between your thumb and second finger like this:

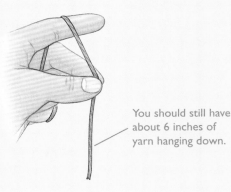

You should still have about 6 inches of yarn hanging down.

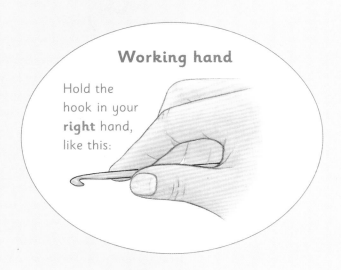

Working hand

Hold the hook in your **right** hand, like this:

...and pinch it between your thumb and second finger like this:

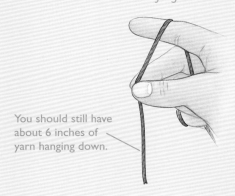

You should still have about 6 inches of yarn hanging down.

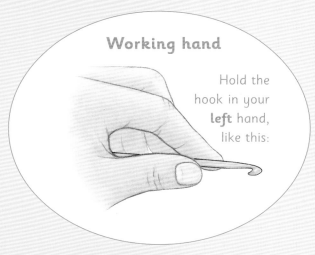

Working hand

Hold the hook in your **left** hand, like this:

The rest of the instructions are written for right-handed crocheters. Lefties, simply reverse the instructions to make them work for you.

Foundation chain

Once you know how to hold your hands, you're ready to start crocheting. Every project starts with a simple chain. Here's how you make one.

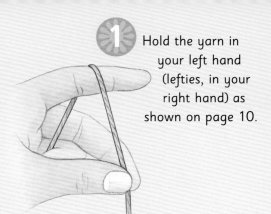

1 Hold the yarn in your left hand (lefties, in your right hand) as shown on page 10.

4 ...like this:

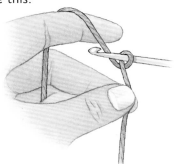

5 Pinch the bottom of the loop to hold it in place, then reach your hook up and pick up the yarn that runs down off your first finger.

Pinch here.

7 ...like so:

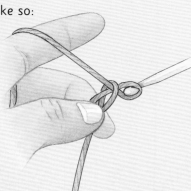

8 Turn your hook so it faces up. You've just made one chain and are ready to make the next one.

2 Now lay your crochet hook on top of the yarn with the hook facing down.

3 Pull your hook down, toward yourself then back up to loop the yarn around the hook...

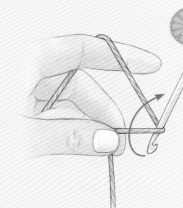

6 Turn your hook so it faces down and pull this yarn through the loop...

Don't be surprised if your first chain doesn't look just right. It takes a little practice before your stitches are neat and even like in the picture.

9 Repeat steps 5–8 until you've made as many stitches as you need.

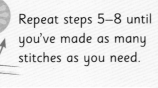

Keep your loops a little loose. This is about the right size.

13

Single crochet

The first stitch you're going to learn is the single crochet. It's the shortest, simplest stitch.

Follow the directions on the next four pages to make a small practice piece. It's the best way to learn. You can keep this practice piece forever, or you can unravel it and reuse the yarn to make a project. Always work with fresh yarn when you're learning a new stitch.

1 To make a practice piece 12 stitches wide, start by making a foundation of **13 chain stitches.**

The first single crochet will go in the **second stitch** from your hook (it's purple in the picture).

13 stitches

3 ...so you have **two loops** on your hook. Perfect.

4 Pick up the yarn with your hook and pull it through **both loops** on your hook.

6 The last stitch can be a little tricky. If you pulled the first stitch of your foundation chain too tight, it will be hard to get your hook into it to make the last stitch.

If this happens, simply loosen the first stitch a bit so you can make the last stitch.

too tight

just right

Turning chain

At the end of every row, you have to make a **turning chain.** This is simply a chain that brings your work up to the height of the next row so that your edges stay nice and straight. The length of the chain is different for each stitch. For the single crochet, the turning chain is **1 chain stitch.**

14

2 Push your hook into the stitch and pick up the yarn like so:

Now pull the yarn through the **first loop** on your hook...

5 You'll be left with **one loop** and you've just finished your first single crochet.

The next stitch goes here.

Make a **single crochet** in the next stitch and in every stitch to the end of the row.

7 Count to be sure you have 12 stitches, then make **1 chain stitch** as the turning chain.

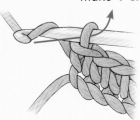

Now, without moving your hook, turn your work over so it's to the left of the hook again (lefties, to the right). Turn the page to see what this looks like.

Tension

One of the hardest things about learning to crochet is getting the tension right. Most beginners tend to crochet too tightly. To keep your stitches from pulling too tight, pinch the bottom of the loops you're working on to hold them in place as you pull the yarn through.

Pinch here.

Use the first finger of your working hand to guide the yarn on the hook as you work.

You'll learn more about tension, also called gauge, on page 30.

Counting stitches

To count your stitches, simply look at the top edge of your work. Every chain stitch represents a stitch.

1 2 3 4 5 6 7 8 9 10 11 12

It's a good idea to count the stitches at the end of each row when you're learning. It's easy to miss the last stitch.

Second row

The only difference between the first row of crochet and the second is where you place your hook in the stitch.

1 Check to be sure your crochet looks like the picture, then start the second row. You're going to skip the turning chain and make the first **single crochet** in the **second stitch** from the hook. It's purple in the picture.

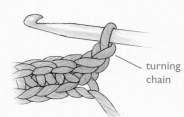

turning chain

4 Now pull the yarn through the **two loops** to finish the single crochet as always.

Push your hook under both loops of the stitch.

5 Make a **single crochet** in the next stitch and in every stitch to the end of the row.

8 Work as many rows as it takes for you to feel comfortable with single crochet.

If you want to save your practice piece, you can cut the end and tie it off as shown in the next few steps. Otherwise, you can unravel your work and wind the yarn into a ball to use again.

Tying off

To tie off, cut the yarn so it's about 6 inches (15 cm) long, then pull it all the way through the last stitch.

6"

2

Push your hook under **both loops** of the stitch as shown.

Pick up the yarn and pull it through **both loops** of the stitch...

3

...so you have **two loops** on your hook.

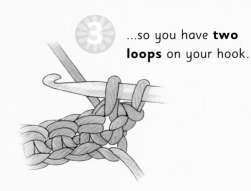

6

Before you make the turning chain, count to be sure you have 12 stitches. If you don't, you may have missed the last one. This is easy to do as it often rolls back a bit.

Make the last stitch here.

7

When you've finished the row, **chain 1** to make the turning chain. Turn your work so it's to the left of your hook and you're ready to start the next row.

Pull the end tight to tighten the knot.

Single crochet details

The foundation chain is always one stitch longer than the number of stitches you want in the first row.

The turning chain is one chain stitch.

On the second and all following rows, the first single crochet is made in the second stitch from your hook.

Half double crochet

This stitch is a little taller than the single crochet but it's just as easy. It makes a slightly softer, looser fabric than the single crochet does. It's used to make the flower and the bath bag.

You'll do best if you start a new practice piece to learn this stitch.

1 To make a practice piece 12 stitches wide, start by making a foundation of **14 chain stitches.**

5 Pick up the yarn again and pull it through **all three loops** on your hook.

6 You just made your first half double crochet. It will look like this:

Your next stitch goes right here.

Now wrap the yarn around your hook again and make a **half double crochet** in the next stitch and in every stitch to the end of the row.

8 Skip the turning chain and make a **half double crochet** in the **third stitch** from your hook, then in every stitch to the end of the row.

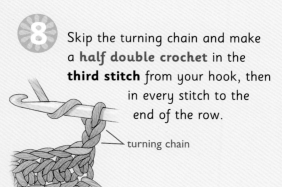

turning chain

9 Count to be sure you have 12 stitches. If you have too few, you probably missed the last one. If you have too many, go back to step 8 to be sure you made the first stitch in the right place.

The last stitch goes here.

Wrap the yarn around your hook one time as shown.

The first half double crochet will go in the **third stitch** from your hook (it's purple in the picture).

Your first stitch goes here.

 Push your hook into the stitch, pick up the yarn and pull it back through the **first loop** on your hook...

 ...so you have **three loops** on your hook.

 Count to be sure you have 12 stitches, then **chain 2** to make the turning chain. Turn your work over and you're ready to start the next row.

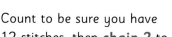

Half double crochet details

The foundation chain is always two stitches longer than the number of stitches you want in the first row.

The turning chain is two chain stitches.

On the second and all following rows, the first half double crochet is made in the third stitch from your hook.

 Crochet as many rows as it takes to feel comfortable with the half double crochet. When you're finished, tie this piece off or unravel it and wind the yarn into a ball to use again.

Double crochet

This stitch is even taller than the half double crochet. It's the most commonly used stitch, so it's important that you learn how to make it.

Once again, start a new practice piece to learn this stitch.

The double crochet is different from the other stitches you've learned so far. Here the turning chain counts as the first double crochet. So if you're making a piece 12 stitches wide, you'll actually only make 11 double crochets. This will make more sense once you work through the steps.

4 ...so you have **three loops** on your hook.

5 Pick up the yarn again and pull it through the **first two loops** on your hook.

6 You'll have **two loops** left on your hook.

9 Count to be sure you have 12 stitches. Count the first 3 chain stitches in the row as the first double crochet. This will be followed by 11 double crochets.

Chain 3 to make the turning chain, then turn your work over.

10 Skip the turning chain and the next stitch. Make a **double crochet** in the **fifth stitch** from your hook, then in every stitch to the end of the row.

Your first stitch goes here.

This is a little different from the stitches you've learned so far.

1 To make a practice piece 12 stitches wide, start by making a foundation of **14 chain stitches**.

2 Wrap the yarn around your hook **one time**.

The first double crochet will go in the **fourth stitch** from your hook.

The first stitch goes here.

3 Push your hook into the stitch, pick up the yarn and pull it back through the **first loop** on your hook...

7 Pick up the yarn once more and pull it through the **last two loops**.

8 You've just made a double crochet. It will look like this:

Wrap the yarn around your hook again and make a **double crochet** in the next stitch and in every stitch to the end of the row.

On your first row, these 3 chain stitches count as the first double crochet.

Note

The last double crochet goes in the top stitch of the turning chain that started the previous row.

There will be a little gap here.

Don't be surprised to see a little gap between the turning chain and the double crochet next to it. This is right.

11 Crochet as many rows as it takes to feel comfortable with the double crochet. When you're finished, tie this piece off or unravel it and wind the yarn into a ball to use again.

Double crochet details

The foundation chain is always two stitches longer than the number of stitches you want in the first row.

The turning chain is three chain stitches long and counts as your first double crochet.

On the second and all following rows, the first double crochet is made in the fifth stitch from your hook.

Triple crochet

This is the tallest stitch yet. You'll probably never make a whole piece out of triple crochet, so don't worry too much about remembering how to start and end the rows just right.

Start a new practice piece to learn this stitch.

 To make a practice piece 12 stitches wide, start by making a foundation of **15 chain stitches.**

 Now pick up the yarn again and pull it through the **first two loops** on your hook.

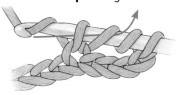

 You'll have **three loops** left on your hook.

 Pick up the yarn again and pull it through the **next two loops**...

 Count to be sure you have 12 stitches. The first 4 chain stitches in the row count as the first triple crochet. It will be followed by 11 triple crochets. **Chain 4** to make the turning chain, then turn your work over.

The first stitch goes here.

Skip the turning chain and the next stitch. Make a **triple crochet** in the **sixth stitch** from your hook, then in every stitch to the end of the row.

22

Wrap the yarn around your hook **two times.** The first triple crochet will go in the **fifth** stitch from your hook.

 The first stitch goes here.

 Push your hook into this stitch, pick up the yarn and pull it through the **first loop**...

 ...so you have **four loops** on your hook.

 ...so there are just **two loops** left on your hook.

 Finally pull the yarn through the **last two loops**...

 ...and you've finished a triple crochet.

Make a triple crochet in the next stitch and in every stitch to the end of the row.

These 4 stitches count as the first triple crochet.

Note

The last triple crochet goes in the top stitch of the turning chain that started the previous row.

 The last stitch goes here.

 Crochet as many rows as it takes to feel comfortable with the triple crochet. When you're finished, tie this piece off or unravel it and wind the yarn into a ball to use again.

Triple crochet details

The foundation chain is always three stitches longer than the number of stitches you want in the first row.

The turning chain is four chain stitches long and counts as the first triple crochet.

On the second and all following rows, the first triple crochet is made in the sixth stitch from the hook.

Slip stitch

The slip stitch is used to join rounds or to move the yarn from one place in your work to another without cutting it. While it may not seem like much on its own, it's a simple little stitch that makes bigger things possible.

1 When a slip stitch is called for, simply push your hook into the stitch indicated in the pattern....

2 ...pick up the yarn and pull it through all of the loops on your hook...

3 ...so you're left with one loop. It's that easy.

Tying off

One of the last things you do when you finish a crochet project is tie the yarn off. This is done the same way no matter what stitch you're using.

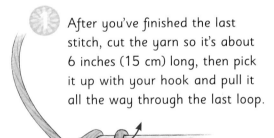

After you've finished the last stitch, cut the yarn so it's about 6 inches (15 cm) long, then pick it up with your hook and pull it all the way through the last loop.

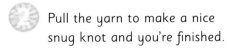

Pull the yarn to make a nice snug knot and you're finished.

Adding yarn

Sooner or later you're going to run out of yarn in the middle of a project. Or you'll want to change colors. In both cases, you'll need to know how to add yarn. While it's possible to add yarn in the middle of a row, it's always better to do it at the end of a row if you can. Here's how:

Work the last stitch until there are just two loops left on your hook (three if it's a half double crochet). Be sure that there are at least 6 inches (15 cm) of the old yarn remaining.

Pull the new yarn through the remaining loops to finish the stitch. Leave a 6-inch (15-cm) tail on the new yarn as well.

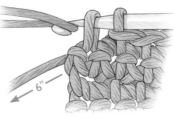

If you're in the middle of a row, simply continue to crochet using the new yarn.

If you're at the end of a row, make your turning chain with the new yarn...

...then continue to crochet using the new yarn.

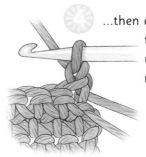

Sewing seams

Several of the projects in this book need to be sewn together. There are a lot of different ways to do this but a simple whip stitch will work well for all of the projects. When you're sewing your crochet together, be sure to use a yarn needle like the one that comes with this book.

Always leave a 6-inch (15-cm) tail on your sewing-up yarn so you can weave the end into your work later. You'll learn how to do this on the next page.

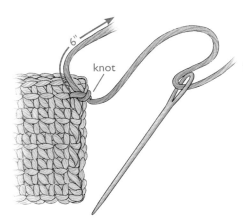

Thread some yarn onto your needle, then pull it almost all the way through the two layers that you're joining. Tie a nice tight knot as shown.

Now make simple whip stitches by pushing your needle up from the bottom to the top, stitching through both layers.

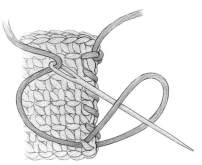

When you're finished, make one more stitch and push your needle through it to make a knot.

Weaving your yarn in

At the end of every project, you'll have at least a couple of loose ends of yarn hanging off. Hide these ends by weaving them into your work.

Whenever you start a project or add yarn, be sure to leave a 6-inch (15-cm) tail of yarn. This gives you plenty of yarn to thread onto your needle and weave into your work.

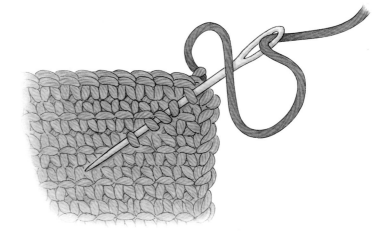

Thread the loose yarn onto your yarn needle and weave it through some stitches on the back of your work. Weave in at least 3 inches (8 cm), then trim the yarn short.

Blocking your work

What is blocking?

Blocking is simply a way to get the final shape of your project just right and to smooth out uneven stitches a bit. You do it after you've finished crocheting your project.

When to block?

Most of the projects in this book don't need to be blocked. Projects made of acrylic yarn don't need to be blocked. But if you've crocheted something using a natural fiber and it isn't shaped quite right, blocking will help.

How to block:

There are a lot of different ways to block your work. Here's an easy way that works especially well for small projects.

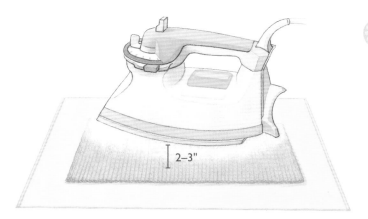

2–3"

1 Lay your finished work down on a thick towel or a couple of towels laid on top of each other. You can block a project before it's assembled or after.

2 Now hold a steaming iron a couple of inches (at least 5 cm) away from your work and steam the whole thing. Never let the iron touch the yarn.

3 Set the iron aside and gently smooth your crocheted piece to shape it. It sometimes helps to pin your work to the towel after you've steamed it so that it holds its shape as it dries.

Gauge

When you start looking at crochet patterns, you'll see that they all specify a gauge. **Gauge is simply the number of stitches per inch of crochet.** Measuring your gauge is important when you're making something that has to be sized just right, like a hat. If you crochet too tightly, your hat will be too small. Too loosely, and it will be too big.

Checking your gauge is easy. Always check your gauge over 4 inches (10 cm). Because the edges of your work can be a little uneven, make a sample piece about 5 inches (13 cm) wide and a couple of rows long. Be sure to work in the stitch specified by the pattern. Lay your work flat, place a ruler on top of it and count the stitches across a span of 4 inches in the middle of a row.

The yarn that comes with this book has a gauge of 4 single crochets per inch. That means you should count 16 stitches over 4 inches (10 cm).

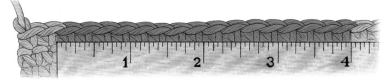

If you have fewer than 16 stitches, try working a little tighter OR try using a slightly smaller crochet hook.

If you have more than 16 inches, your gauge is a little tight. Try working your stitches a little looser OR try using a slightly larger crochet hook.

Remember, for most of the projects in this book, getting close to the right gauge is good enough.

It's not important that your gauge be exactly right for any project except the hat. Still, it's a good idea to check your gauge as you're learning, just to be sure you're on the right track.

Buying more yarn

The first time you walk into a yarn store, you may feel a little overwhelmed. You'll see yarn in different weights, different materials, different textures, not to mention all the different colors. **Don't panic**. Finding the right yarn is easier than it seems. Yarn comes in a variety of weights (sport, DK, worsted, bulky, etc.). Each weight has a different gauge and will be worked with a different size hook. When you're buying yarn for a project, look for something that is the same weight as the yarn your pattern calls for. This should get you to the right gauge. Here are some more tips for finding the right yarn.

Tips for buying yarn

✳ All of the projects in this book are made with DK (double knit) weight yarn. Look for this weight when you shop for more yarn. The soap bag can be made with either DK or a slightly lighter yarn.

✳ Yarn stores usually organize their yarn by weight, so you can simply tell the salesperson what you're looking for and they'll point you in the right direction.

✳ Most patterns call for a specific brand of yarn. Don't let this throw you. You can use any yarn that's the same weight as the yarn called for.

✳ If you're still not sure what to buy, just ask. People who work in yarn stores are used to helping people find the right yarn. Even experienced crocheters ask for help. Really.

Reading labels

The information printed on yarn labels varies from yarn to yarn. If you're lucky, you'll find something like this:

This tells you that the yarn is DK weight.

This number tells you what size crochet hook to use with the yarn.

The **8 UK** and **US 6** tell knitters what size needles to use.

• Some labels will show a picture of a crochet hook with the correct size noted. Easy.

• If you only see knitting-needle size noted, you're probably still ok. When a 4.0 mm knitting needle is called for, look for a crochet hook of the same size.

Real-world crochet

Once you've worked through the projects in this book, you're ready to take on just about any crochet pattern. Even the most complex stitch combinations are made up of the basic stitches you've already learned.

When you pick up other books or patterns, you'll see that they're written in a kind of crochet code. There will be a lot of abbreviations. There will be very few full sentences. You'll probably find it all a little intimidating. **Don't.**

Remember: You know the basics. And just about every pattern will include a guide telling you what each abbreviation stands for. Just in case you need them, you'll find a list of common abbreviations to the right.

beg	beginning	sc	single crochet
ch	chain	sk	skip
dc	double crochet	sl st	slip stitch
dec	decrease	sp	space
hdc	half double crochet	st	stitch
inc	increase	tog	together
lp	loop	tr	triple crochet
rnd	round	yo	yarn over*

* **Yarn over** is simply another way of telling you to wrap the yarn around your hook.

Hook placement

You've learned to crochet by pushing your hook under both loops of each stitch. You'll find some patterns that ask you to work into the front or back loop only. The picture to the right will show you what this means.

Try working some practice rows to see what it looks like when you push your hook through a different part of the stitch.

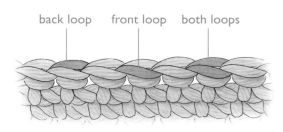

back loop   front loop   both loops

Crochet in the UK

The crochet terms used in this book are from the United States. If you're buying patterns or books in the UK, you'll find a whole different set of terms. Don't worry. The stitches are the same, it's just the names that are different.

Here's a quick cheat sheet to help you translate.

US	UK
single crochet	double crochet (dc)
half double crochet	half treble crochet (htr)
double crochet	treble crochet (tr)
triple crochet	double treble crochet (dtr)
slip stitch	slip stitch (sl st)

Measurements in the UK are always metric.

One last bit of advice

If you ask three different crocheters how to do something, you may well get three different answers. Don't be put off by this. If someone shows you a different way of doing something, give it a try. It might just work better for you.

Remember, if it works, it's right.

Projects

Once you've worked through the basics of crochet and feel pretty comfortable with the different stitches, you're ready to make one of the projects. The first three are the quickest and the easiest to complete. Start with one of these and you'll be an expert by the time you get to the larger projects.

Jewelry Roll

This is the perfect project to make first. It's easy and beautiful. Crochet the first one for yourself, then make more to give as gifts.

If you know how to make a single crochet, you're ready to start.

What You Need

4.0 mm crochet hook

50 yards (45 m) of DK yarn

yarn needle

This is a great time to work on getting your gauge right. The gauge for the yarn that comes with this book is 4 single crochets per inch (2.5 cm). So if you're on target, your jewelry roll will measure about 5 inches (13 cm) across. For this project (and for most in this book) close is good enough.

1 Start by making a chain of 21 stitches. Then make a **single crochet** in the second stitch from the hook. It's darker in the picture.

The first single crochet goes here.

2 Perfect. Now make a **single crochet** in the next stitch and in every stitch to the end of the row.

The next single crochet goes here.

3 Count to be sure you have 20 stitches, then **chain 1** to make a turning chain.

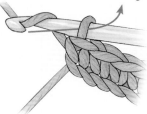

4 Turn your work over. Repeat the instructions in the box until your piece is 7 inches (18 cm) long. It doesn't have to be exact.

The first stitch goes here.

- Make a **single crochet** in the second stitch from the hook, and then in every stitch to the end of the row.
- Count to be sure you have 20 stitches.
- **Chain 1.**
- Turn your work over.

Now you're ready to assemble your roll. It's easy.

7 Lay your work down flat so that the long end of yarn is at the bottom. Fold the bottom edge up 2 inches (5 cm) to make a little pocket.

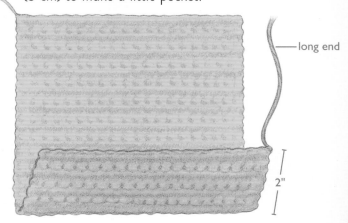

long end

2"

5

Your jewelry roll will look like this:

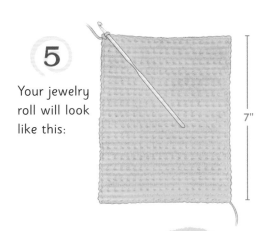

7"

6 Cut the end of the yarn so it's about 10 inches (25 cm) long, and pull it all the way through the last stitch to tie off.

10"

8 Thread the long end of yarn onto your yarn needle and use a whip stitch to sew the edges of the folded-up pocket together.

9 Knot your yarn and weave it into the inside of the pocket.

Thread your needle with another piece of yarn and sew up the other side of the pocket in the same way.

Weave all the loose ends of yarn into your work.

Forgot how to weave in? Go to page 28 for a reminder.

11 Turn your bag over so the pocket is face down. Use your crochet hook to weave the tie through a couple of rows of crochet at the very center of your piece.

12 Your jewelry roll will look something like this:

10 Now you're ready to make the tie. To do this, simply make a chain about 15 inches (38 cm) long. It can be the same color as your roll, or it can be something different.

Tie it off when it's long enough.

15"

Make a bag for your glasses

Simply start with a foundation chain that's a little longer than your glasses are wide. Work until your piece is as long as it needs to be to make a deep-enough pocket and a long-enough flap.

The bag in the picture started with a foundation chain of 24 stitches and made a bag about 6 inches (15 cm) wide. The flap is just long enough to reach the bottom of the pocket.

Or a bag for your crochet hooks

This bag was a 6-inch (15-cm) square before the pocket was folded up.

13 Pull the ends of your tie really tight, then cut them short. Your bag is ready to use!

Cut here.

Flower

This pretty little flower
is quick and easy to
make. Sew it on a hat,
pin it to your jacket
or tie it to your flip-flops.

You'll need to know the
half double, double and
triple crochet stitches
to make this project.

What You Need

4.0 mm crochet hook

7 yards (6.5 m) of DK yarn

yarn needle

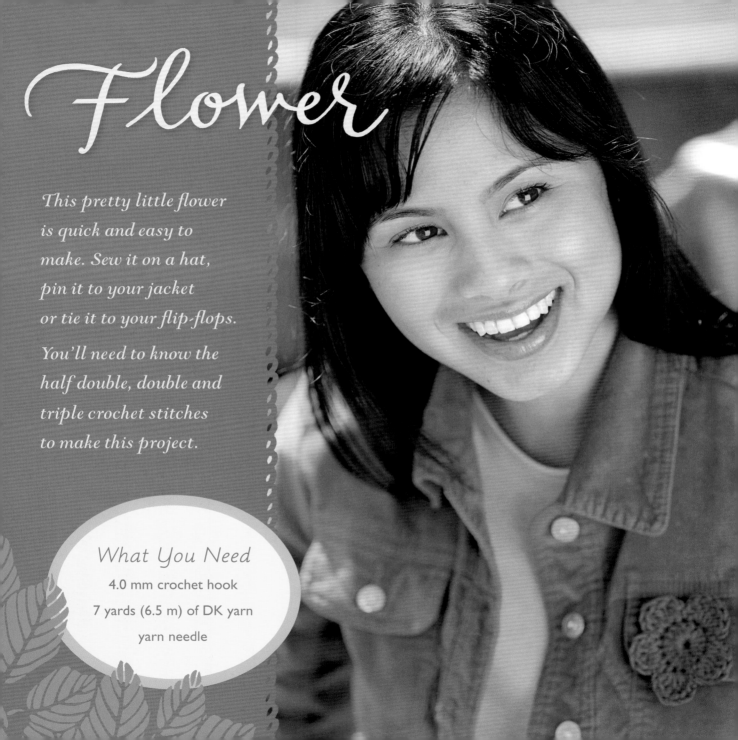

You can make the flower using either of the yarns that come with this book.

1 Start by making a chain of 6 stitches. Next you're going to join the ends of the chain. To do this, push your hook through the first stitch...

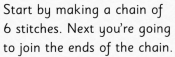

2 ...pick up the yarn and pull it through both loops on your hook.

3 Good. Now **chain 3**.

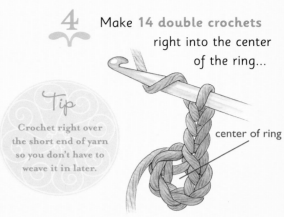

4 Make **14 double crochets** right into the center of the ring...

center of ring

7 Check to be sure your flower looks like the picture. **Chain 1.**

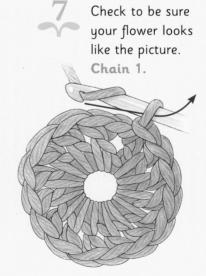

5 ...like so:

Next you're going to join your work into a complete circle with a **slip stitch.** To do this, poke your hook into the space between that string of 3 chains and the first double crochet...

Push your hook into this space.

6 ...pick up the yarn and pull it through both loops on your hook.

8 Now you're ready to start the first petal.

The next 3 stitches go here.

In the next stitch, make these three stitches:

· 1 half double crochet
· 1 double crochet
· 1 triple crochet

9 Good. That's half a petal. Now make the other half.

The next 3 stitches go here.

In the next stitch make:

· 1 triple crochet
· 1 double crochet
· 1 half double crochet

10 To finish your petal, **chain 1.**

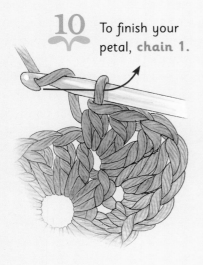

11 Now make a **slip stitch** into the next stitch.

Make a slip stitch right here.

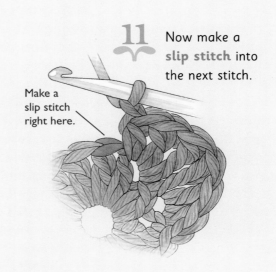

Slip stitch reminder

Push your hook under the next stitch, pick up the yarn and pull it all the way through both loops on your hook.

12 Repeat steps 7–11 to make a total of 5 petals.

Make a **slip stitch** into the last stitch...

Tie a flower to your flip-flop.

...or onto the strap of your bag.

You can even sew one onto your granny square scarf.

13 ...then cut the end of the yarn so it's about 6 inches (15 cm) long. Pull it all the way through the last stitch to tie off.

Weave the loose ends of yarn into the back of your flower. Very nice.

Bath Bag

Tuck a bar of nicely scented soap into this bag and use it like a wash cloth to gently cleanse your skin in the bath or shower. When you're finished, simply hang it to dry until you're ready to use it again.

You'll need to know how to make a double crochet and a half double crochet to make this bag.

What You Need

4.0 mm crochet hook

30 yards (27 m) of DK or slightly lighter yarn

yarn needle

Use the light-weight yarn that comes with this book for this project. If you want to make more bath bags, look for mercerized cotton in a sport or DK weight. This will make the prettiest bag.

1 Start by making a chain of 29 stitches. Your chain should be about 6 inches (15 cm) long.

Make a **double crochet** in the fourth stitch from the hook and in every stitch to the end of the row.

Your first double crochet goes here.

2 Perfect. This time, don't make any turning stitches.

3 Circle your work around so that the beginning of the row is next to the end. Look at the picture to be sure you've got it right.

Now find the little space just before the first double crochet. Look at the picture for help.

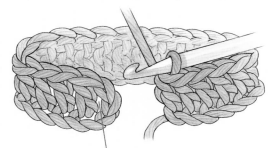

Your next stitch will go into this space.

49

Tie a bath bag and a bar of scented soap together for a pretty little gift.

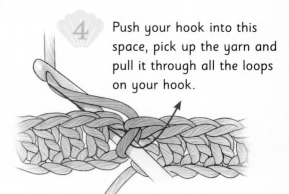

4 Push your hook into this space, pick up the yarn and pull it through all the loops on your hook.

7 Chain 1.

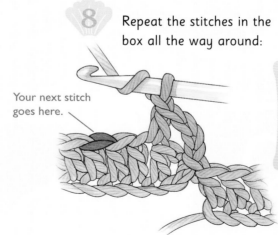

8 Repeat the stitches in the box all the way around:

Your next stitch goes here.

• Skip a stitch.
• Make a **half double crochet** in the next stitch.
• Chain 1.

5 Now **chain 3.**

6 Good. You're ready to start the pattern. Skip a stitch and make a **half double crochet** in the next one.

Your next stitch goes here.

When you crochet in a circle like this, it's called *working in the round.*

Push your hook into this big space to make the next stitch.

9 When you've circled back to where you started, you've finished the first round.

Continue with the pattern, but from here on out make each half double crochet in the next big space in the previous row. Remember to make 1 chain stitch between each half double crochet.

This is your pattern now:

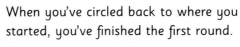

• Make a **half double crochet** in the next big space in the previous row.

• **Chain 1.**

51

10

Crochet around and around until your bag is about an inch (2.5 cm) longer than your bar of soap, and the last stitch is almost directly above the little gap in your first row. End with a chain stitch.

11

Make a **single crochet** into the next big space.

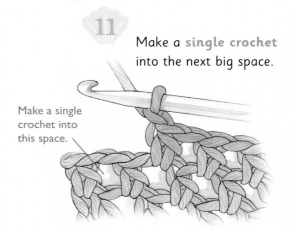

Make a single crochet into this space.

12

Now you're ready to close up the bottom of your bag. To do this, turn your bag so it's to the left of your hook and hold the front and back edges together.

13

Push your hook through the nearest stitch on both the front and back edges, pick up the yarn and pull it through all the loops on your hook.

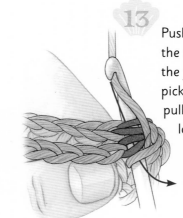

14 Your bag will look like this:

Repeat step 13 all the way across to close up the bottom of the bag.

15 Once you've worked all the way across, cut the yarn so it's about 6 inches (15 cm) long and pull it through the last stitch to tie off.

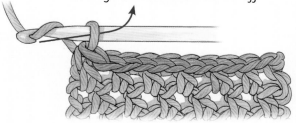

Weave the loose ends of yarn into your work, and then turn the bag inside-out to hide the slip stitches.

17 Thread the end of yarn on the drawstring through your yarn needle and weave it through the stitches all the way around the bag.

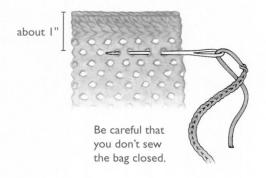

about 1"

Be careful that you don't sew the bag closed.

18 Tie the drawstring in a half knot close to the bag, but don't cinch it closed until you've put the soap in the bag.

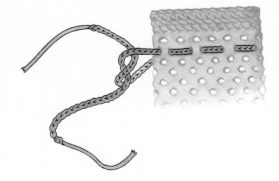

16 Now make a chain about 10 inches (25 cm) long. This will be your drawstring. Leave about 4 inches (10 cm) of yarn at the end.

19 Finally, tie the ends of the drawstring together in a knot so it's easy to hang your bag in the shower. Cut the ends short. Beautiful.

After you've used up a bar of soap, rinse the bag and let it dry completely before filling it with new soap.

Envelope Purse

This handy little purse is made with a simple combination of stitches that ends up looking much more complex than it is. That's the beauty of crochet.

You need only know the single and double crochet to make this project.

What You Need

4.0 mm crochet hook

70 yards (63 m) of DK yarn

yarn needle

1 Start by making a
chain of 25 stitches.
Make a **single crochet**
in the second stitch
from the hook...

The first
single crochet
goes here.

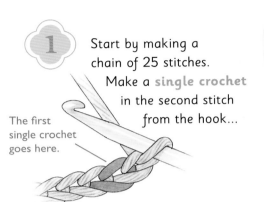

2 ...and in every stitch
to the end of the row.

The second
single crochet
goes here.

3 Count your stitches to be
sure you have 24. **Chain 1**
to make a turning chain.

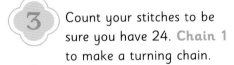

4 The pretty — but simple — pattern starts with the second row. Here's how it goes: Make **1 single crochet** in the second stitch from the hook.

Make a single crochet here.

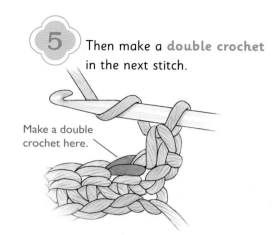

5 Then make a **double crochet** in the next stitch.

Make a double crochet here.

If you work your pattern correctly, the last stitch in every row will be a double crochet. If this isn't the case, simply unravel your work as far as your mistake and rework it correctly.

7 **Chain 1** to make a turning chain then turn your work over to start the next row.

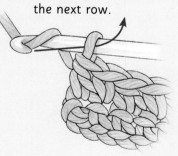

8 Repeat steps 4–7, crocheting each row just like you did the last one.

The first single crochet goes here.

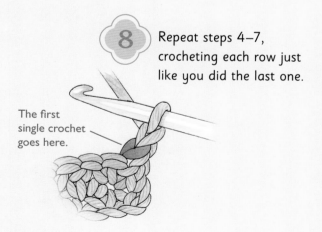

6 Repeat the stitches in the box all the way to the end of the row.

- 1 single crochet
- 1 double crochet

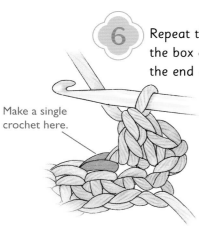

Make a single crochet here.

9 You'll get a very pretty, slightly irregular pattern. It will look very complicated. Only you will know how easy it is.

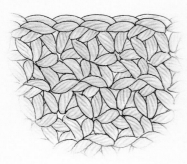

10 Work like this until your piece measures 7 inches (18 cm). It's okay if it's not exact.

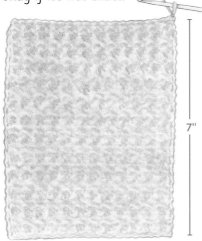

7"

 11 Make 3 rows of single crochet.

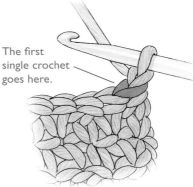

The first single crochet goes here.

13 Continue to make a **single crochet** in every stitch until there are only two stitches remaining. Skip a stitch and make a **single crochet** in the very last stitch.

Count to be sure you have 22 stitches now.

Don't forget to make a turning stitch at the end of each row.

Tip

Identifying the last stitch can get a little tricky once you start decreasing. You'll do best if you count the stitches in each row as you work just to be sure you've got it right. Each row will have two stitches fewer than the previous row.

12 Now you're ready to start shaping the flap. You do this by making a **decrease** at the beginning and end of each row. It's much easier than it sounds. Instead of making your first single crochet in the second stitch from your hook, make it in the third.

The first single crochet goes here.

14 Repeat steps 12 and 13, making decreases until there are only 4 stitches remaining. Your flap will look like this:

Perfect.

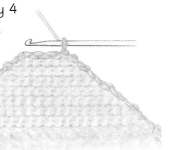

The sides of your flap will slant toward the center as you make your decreases.

15 Now **chain 3**. This is the start of the buttonhole.

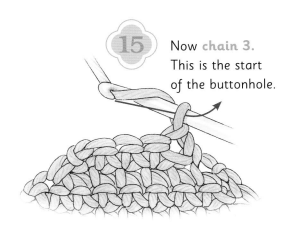

16 Finish the buttonhole by making a **slip stitch** in the last stitch of the row.

Make a slip stitch right here.

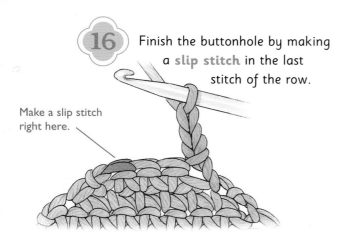

17 Cut the end of your yarn so it's about 6 inches (15 cm) long then pull it through the last stitch to tie off.

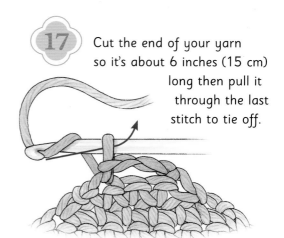

20 Next you're going make a row of **single crochet** along the edge of your flap to finish it nicely. To do this, push your hook into the hole at the end of the next row...

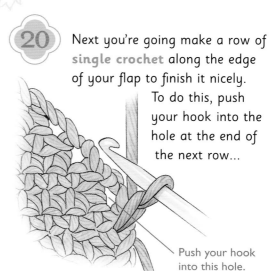

Push your hook into this hole.

18 Now find the first row of single crochet where your flap starts. Pull a new loop of yarn through the edge of this row. This yarn can be the same color as your purse, or it can be something different.

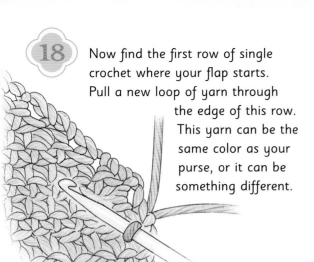

19 Chain 1.

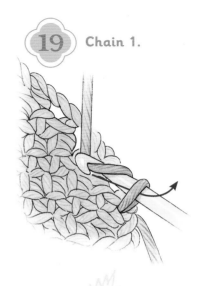

21 ...then pick up the yarn and pull it through...

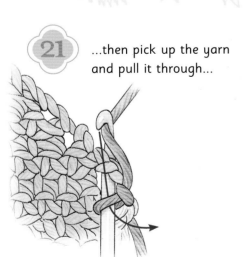

22 ...so you have two loops on your hook. Pick up the yarn again and pull it through both loops. You've finished your first single crochet.

23 Repeat steps 20–22 all the way up the side of your flap. When you get to the tip, make **3 single crochets** in the buttonhole.

Make 3 single crochets into this space.

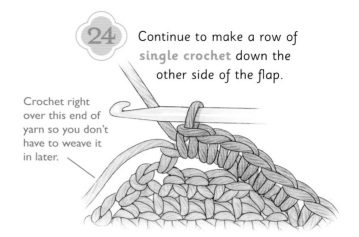

24 Continue to make a row of **single crochet** down the other side of the flap.

Crochet right over this end of yarn so you don't have to weave it in later.

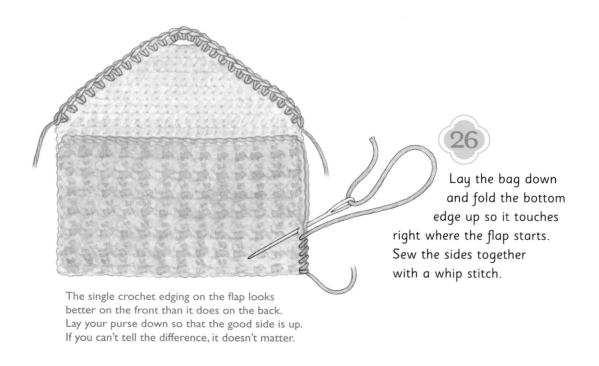

26 Lay the bag down and fold the bottom edge up so it touches right where the flap starts. Sew the sides together with a whip stitch.

The single crochet edging on the flap looks better on the front than it does on the back. Lay your purse down so that the good side is up. If you can't tell the difference, it doesn't matter.

25 When you get to the bottom of the flap, cut the end of the yarn so it's about 6 inches (15 cm) long and pull it all the way through to tie off.

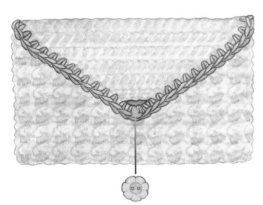

Sew the button to the front of your purse right under the buttonhole.

27

Turn the bag inside out to hide the stitches, then fold the flap down to see where the button wants to be.

Sew the button on the bag using an ordinary needle and thread. Be careful not to sew your bag closed.

Weave in all the loose ends of yarn.

Hat

This hat, with its pretty scalloped trim, is actually quite easy to make. It's worked in the round, so there's no seam to sew up. Make the hat all one color, or choose a different color for the scallop.

You'll need to know both single and double crochet.

What You Need

4.0 mm crochet hook

115 yards (104 m) of DK yarn

stitch marker

yarn needle

The hat is the one project in this book where gauge matters. If you crochet too tightly, your hat may turn out too small. Too loosely, and it may turn out too big.

The correct gauge for this hat is 13–14 double crochets over 4 inches (10 cm). Turn to page 30 if you need help checking your gauge.

1 Start by making a chain of 4 stitches. Join the ends by making a **slip stitch** in the first stitch...

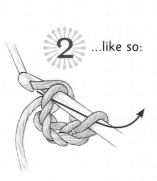

2 ...like so:

3 You'll have a little ring of yarn. **Chain 3.**

Keep the short end of yarn close to your work and crochet right over it so you don't have to weave it in later.

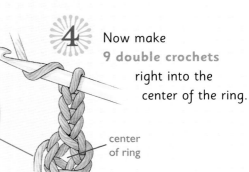

4 Now make **9 double crochets** right into the center of the ring.

center of ring

You'll be making increases to your hat over the next five rounds. This simply means you'll be adding stitches. Find a quiet place where you can crochet uninterrupted while you're working these rounds. Increasing isn't difficult, but you have to count your stitches carefully as you work.

Make 2 double crochets into this space.

5 Find one of your stitch markers and slip it onto the stitch that's on your hook. Check the picture to be sure you've got it right.

Now make **2 double crochets** into the space between that first string of chains and the first double crochet.

If you can't find your stitch markers, a small safety pin will work just as well.

 **6** It will look like this:

Now make **2 double crochets** in the next stitch and in every stitch around. Stop when you get to the stitch marker.

There should be 9 stitches between your hook and the stitch marker.

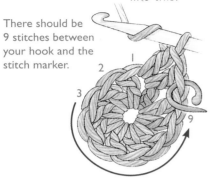

7 You've just finished the second round. Starting with the stitch with your marker on it, count to be sure you have 20 stitches.

8 Move your marker to the loop on your hook, then repeat the stitches in the purple box all the way around.

Make a double crochet here.

- **1 double crochet** in the next stitch
- **2 double crochets** in the following stitch

9 Stop when you get to your marker. Count to be sure you have 30 stitches now.

10 Move your marker to the loop on your hook and start the 4th round. Repeat the stitches in the box all the way around. They're different from the last round.

Make a double crochet here.

- **1 double crochet** in the next 2 stitches
- **2 double crochets** in the following stitch

11 Stop when you come to your marker. Count to be sure you have 40 stitches now.

Tip

The last stitch in every round should have 2 double crochets in it. If it doesn't, you probably miscounted. You'll have to unravel your work to find your mistake.

14 Move your marker to the loop on your hook, and start the last round of increases. Repeat the stitches in the box all the way around.

Make a double crochet in this stitch.

- **1 double crochet** in the next 4 stitches
- **2 double crochets** in the following stitch

15 Stop when you come to your marker. You should have 60 stitches.

12 Move your marker to the loop on your hook and start the 5th round. Repeat the stitches in the box all the way around.

Make a double crochet in this stitch.

> • **1 double crochet** in the next 3 stitches
> • **2 double crochets** in the following stitch

13 Stop when you come to your marker. You should have 50 stitches.

16 You've finished the hard part. Move your marker down a row so it's out of your way but marks the end of the round. Make a **double crochet** in every stitch around...

Move your stitch marker down a row.

17 ...and around. Stop when your hat is a half inch (1.25 cm) short of long-enough. About 7 inches (18 cm) will be right for most people. Stop more-or-less in line with your stitch marker.

stitch marker

18 You're ready to start the scalloped edge. If you want the trim to be a different color, add new yarn on the next stitch (see page 26). Make a **single crochet** in the next stitch.

Make a single crochet right here.

19 Skip a stitch, then make **5 double crochets** in the next one.

Make 5 double crochets in this stitch.

22 When you get back to the beginning of the round, skip a stitch and make a **slip stitch** in the next one.

23 Cut your yarn so it's about 6 inches (15 cm) long and pull it all the way through the last stitch to tie off. Weave all the loose ends of yarn into your work. Beautiful!

20 Look at the picture to be sure your scallop looks right. Repeat the stitches in the box to work the scallop all the way around.

- Skip a stitch.
- Make a single crochet in the next one.
- Skip a stitch.
- Make 5 double crochets in the next one.

21 Your scalloped edge will look like this:

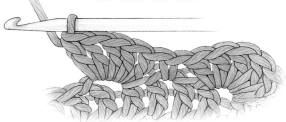

To make the trim a different color, add a new color of yarn as you make the single crochet in step 18. Go to page 26 if you don't remember how to do this.

Granny Square Scarf

This pretty scarf is made up of lots of squares sewn together. You can use the yarn that comes with this book to make the scarf in one color, or head to the yarn store if you want it to be more colorful.

What You Need

4.0 mm crochet hook

215 yards (194 m) of DK yarn

yarn needle

1 Start by making **6 chain stitches**.

Join the ends of the chain with a **slip stitch**. To do this, push your hook into the first stitch...

Push your hook into this stitch.

2 ...then pick up the yarn and pull it through both loops on your hook.

3 You'll have a little ring of chain stitches and are ready to start your first round. **Chain 3.**

Keep the short end of yarn close to the ring and crochet right over it so you won't have to weave it in later.

4 Good. Now make **2 double crochets** right into the center of the ring.

Push your hook into the center of the ring to make 2 double crochets.

5 It will look like this:

Chain 3. These chains will form the first corner of your square.

This group of stitches is called a shell. A shell is usually made up of 3 double crochets, but in your first shell the string of 3 chains counts as a double crochet.

6 Perfect. Now make **3 double crochets** into the center of the ring.

center of ring

Traveling Stitches

Every new round starts in a corner. But if you look at your square now, you'll see that the yarn is just past the corner. To move to the next corner you have to make 3 slip stitches. This is simply a way to move to a different place in your work without cutting the yarn.

9 Make a **slip stitch** in each of the next two stitches...

Make a slip stitch in each of these stitches.

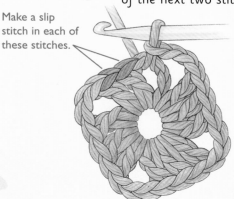

7 Repeat the steps in the box two more times:

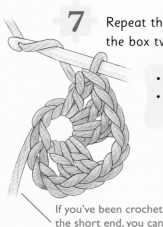

- **Chain 3.**
- Make **3 double crochets** into the center of the ring.

Finish by making **3 chain stitches.**

If you've been crocheting over the short end, you can go ahead and cut it short now.

8 Check to be sure your square looks like the picture. You'll have 4 shells and a chain of 3 stitches coming off your hook. Finish this round by making a **slip stitch** into the space between that first string of 3 chains and the first double crochet.

Make your slip stitch right here.

Slip stitch reminder
Push your hook into the space, pick up the yarn and pull it through all the loops on your hook.

10 ...then make one more **slip stitch** right into the corner hole.

Make the last slip stitch into this hole.

11 Your yarn should be coming right out of the corner.

You've finished the first round and are ready to start the second one.

2nd round

Before you start the second round, look at your square and find the holes at each of the four corners. You're going to crochet into each of these holes as you make the second round.

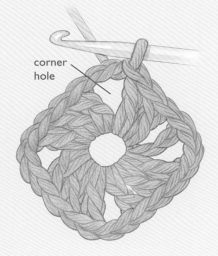

corner hole

Every round of your granny square is made up of the same pieces:

First corner: These are made the same way on every round.

The three other corners: While different from the first corner, these are also made the same way no matter which round you're on.

Sides: The sides of your square get longer with each round.

This will all make more sense once you've made a few rounds.

Make your second round like this:

12 Start with the **first corner**.

- Chain 3.
- Make 2 double crochets into the first corner hole.
- Chain 3.
- Make 3 double crochets into the same corner hole.

13 Make the **side**.

- Chain 1.

14 Then make the next **corner**.

- Make 3 double crochets into the next corner hole.
- Chain 3.
- Make 3 double crochets into the same corner hole.

Start here and work your way around.

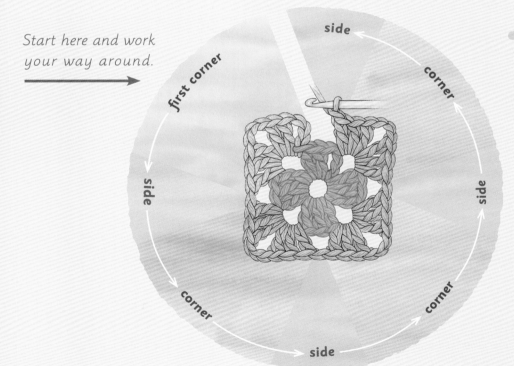

first corner

side

side

corner

corner

side

side

corner

15 Repeat steps 13 and 14 two more times.

Then repeat step 13 again to make the last side.

This picture shows the completed second round. Check it as you work to be sure you're making each section right.

16 Now finish the round by making a **slip stitch** into the gap between the string of three chains and the first double crochet in the next shell.

Make a slip stitch right here.

17 Make a **slip stitch** in each of the next two stitches and then into the corner hole to move your yarn to the corner. This is what you did in steps 9–10, and is done the same way no matter which round you're on.

3rd round

Before you start the third round, look at your square and find the holes at each of the four corners. You'll also see a hole on each side.

You're going to crochet into each of these holes as you make the third round.

Make sure the yarn is coming right out of the first corner before you start this round.

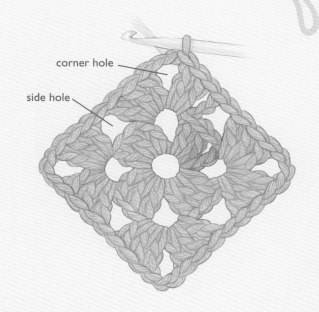

corner hole

side hole

The third round is made just like the second one except that the sides are a little longer.

18 Start with the **first corner**.

- Chain 3.
- Make 2 double crochets into the first corner hole.
- Chain 3.
- Make 3 double crochets into the same corner hole.

19 Then make the **side**.

- Chain 1.
- Make 3 double crochets into the side hole.
- Chain 1.

20 Make the next **corner**.

- Make 3 double crochets into the corner hole.
- Chain 3.
- Make 3 double crochets into the same corner hole.

Start here and work your way around.

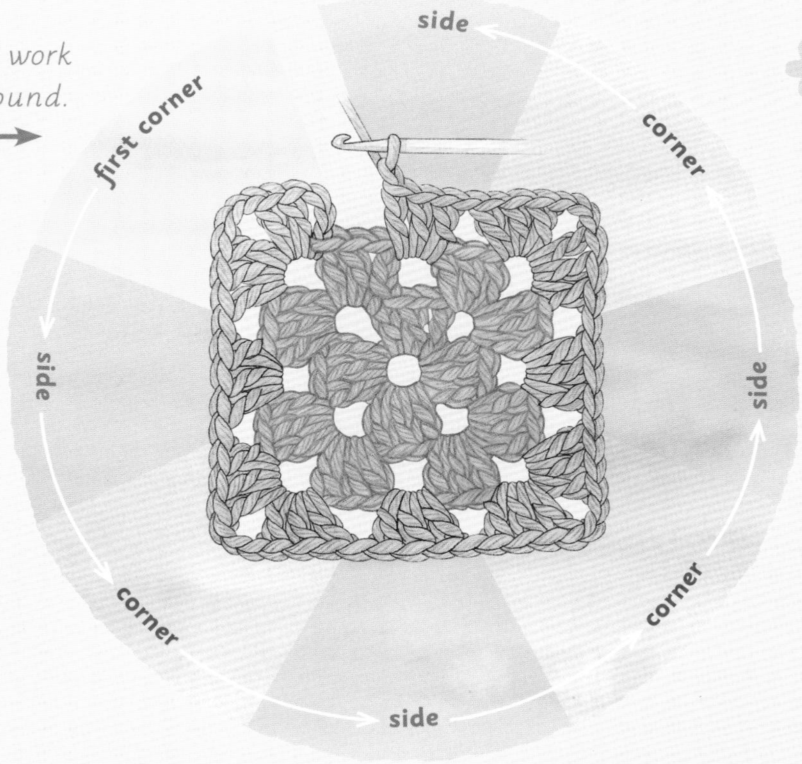

21 Repeat steps 19 and 20 two more times.

Then repeat step 19 once more to make the last side.

This picture shows the completed third round. Check it as you work to be sure you're making each section right.

side

corner

first corner

side

side

corner

corner

side

22 Finish the round by making a **slip stitch** into the gap between the string of three chains and the first double crochet in the next shell.

Make a slip stitch right here.

23 Make a **slip stitch** in each of the next two stitches and then into the corner hole to move your yarn to the corner.

4th round

Before you start the fourth round, look at your square and find the holes at each of the four corners. You'll also see two holes on each side.

You're going to crochet into these holes to make your fourth round.

Make sure the yarn is coming right out of the first corner before you start this round.

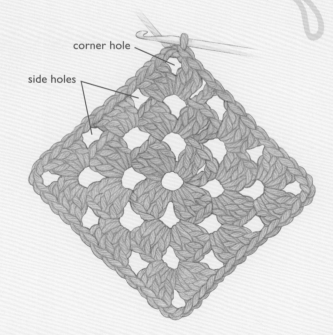

corner hole

side holes

The fourth round is made just like the third one except that the sides are a little longer.

24 Start with the **first corner.**

- Chain 3.
- Make 2 double crochets into the first corner hole.
- Chain 3.
- Make 3 double crochets into the same corner hole.

25 Then make the **side.**

- Chain 1.
- Make 3 double crochets into the first side hole.
- Chain 1.
- Make 3 double crochets into the next side hole.
- Chain 1.

26 Make the next **corner.**

- Make 3 double crochets into the corner hole.
- Chain 3.
- Make 3 double crochets into the same corner hole.

Start here and work your way around.

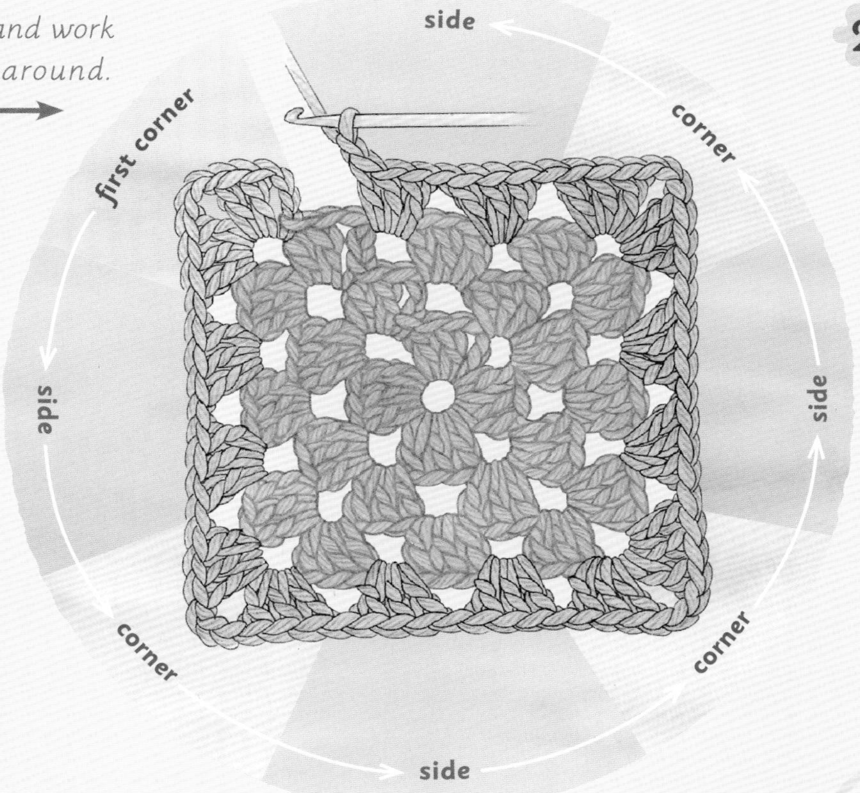

27 Repeat steps 25 and 26 two more times.

Then repeat step 25 once more to make the last side.

This picture shows the completed fourth round. Check it as you work to be sure you're making each section right.

first corner

side

corner

side

side

corner

side

corner

28 Finish the round by making a **slip stitch** into the gap between the string of three chains and the first double crochet in the next shell.

Make a slip stitch right here.

29 Make a **slip stitch** in each of the next two stitches and then into the corner hole to move your yarn to the corner.

30 Cut the end of yarn so it's about 8 inches (20 cm) long and pull it all the way through the last stitch to tie off. You'll use this long end of yarn to sew your squares together.

31 Make eleven squares all together. This will make a scarf about 50 inches (125 cm) long. If you want to add more squares, you'll need about 19 yards (17 m) of yarn to make each square. The squares should measure about 4.5 inches (11.5 cm).

Assembling your scarf

If your squares are each a slightly different size, it's a good idea to block them (see page 29) so they're all the same size.

When you're ready to assemble your scarf, simply line up the edges of two squares, making sure that one (and only one) of them has a long end of yarn hanging off it.

Thread this end onto your yarn needle and stitch the two squares together with a simple whip stitch (see page 27). Weave the end of yarn into your work. Join all the squares just like this.

Adding Fringe

1 Cut a piece of yarn 7 inches (18 cm) long. Fold it in half and use your hook to pull it through the bottom edge of your scarf like so:

7"

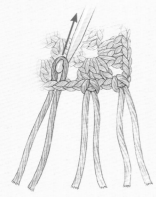

2 Pull the ends of the fringe up through the loop...

3 ...then pull down gently to tighten the knot.

Repeat steps 1–3, using 10 pieces of yarn for each end of the scarf.

Changing colors

It's easy to make each round a different color. Before you add a new color, finish the last round and tie off. You don't have to make those three slip stitches.

1 Pull a new piece of yarn through any corner.

2 Pick up both ends of yarn and pull them through the loop on your hook to make a **chain stitch**.

3 Let the short end of yarn drop and **chain 2** more stitches.

4 Continue to make your first corner as always. If you hold the short end of yarn close to your square and crochet over it as you work, you won't have to weave it in later.

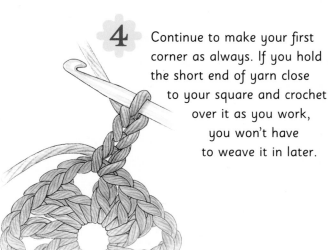

You can make your squares
look completely different
just by changing the way
you use color.

Credits

Book design
Keeli McCarthy

Production design
Maria Corrales

Art direction
Kate Paddock
Jill Turney

Technical illustration
Vally Hennings
Darwen Hennings

Decorative illustration
Keeli McCarthy

Calligraphy
Rosemary Woods

Photography
Katrine Naleid
Peter Fox
Joseph Quever
Judi Swinks

**Button design
and watercolor**
Liz Hutnick

Crochet consultant
Donna Swenson

Production Editor
Jen Mills

Sourcing
Paula Hannigan

Models
Taya Asimos
Missy Broderick
Dawn Cardon
Coreen Collins
Amy Endicott
Elisha Garg
Kristen Gomez
Bailey Griscom
Ericka Harden
Paulabianca Hatter
Lakshmi Karra
Jamie Lease
Miranda Lilley
Meaganne McCanders
Giovannie Pico
Jahvita Rastafari
Tara Pilar Robello
Mia Sakai
Mia Simon
Claire Watt
Katie Yip
Chelsea Young
DeeDee the dog

Special thanks to
Sylvia Reader
Megan Smith
Laura Young
Laurie Campbell
Kathy Harrington
Georgia Herzog
Patty Morris
Rachelle Adams
Hollis Bischoff
 of Full Thread Ahead
and all the new crocheters at Klutz

Can't get enough?

Here are some simple ways to keep the Klutz coming.

1   Get your hands on a copy of The Klutz Catalog. To request
    a free copy of our mail order catalog, go to **klutz.com/catalog**.

2   Become a Klutz Insider and get e-mail about new releases, special offers,
    contests, games, goofiness and who-knows-what-all. If you're a grown-up
    who wants to receive e-mail from Klutz, head to **klutz.com/insider**.

3   If any of this sounds good to you, but you don't feel like going online
    right now, just give us a call at **1-800-737-4123**. We'd love to hear from you.
    www.klutz.com

More great books from Klutz

Knitting
Handmade Cards
Spool Knit Jewelry
Scoubidou
Origami
Twirled Paper
Paper Fashions
Hemp Bracelets
Ribbon Purses
Friendship Bracelets